HD APR 2013
EN JUN 2013

SA JUN 2016

KR Jul 17

SU OCT 2018

HOPING FOR PEACE IN
IRAN

Divided by conflict, wishing for peace

by Jim Pipe

Gareth Stevens
Publishing

Please visit our website, www.garethstevens.com. For a free color catalog of all our high-quality books, call toll free 1-800-542-2595 or fax 1-877-542-2596.

Library of Congress Cataloging-in-Publication Data

Pipe, Jim, 1966-
 Hoping for peace in Iran / Jim Pipe.
    p. cm. — (Peace pen pals)
 Includes index.
ISBN 978-1-4339-7728-2 (pbk.)
ISBN 978-1-4339-7729-9 (6-pack)
ISBN 978-1-4339-7727-5 (library binding)
1. Iran—Juvenile literature. I. Title.
 DS254.75.P56 2013
 955.06—dc23
                                        2012006701

First Edition

Published in 2013 by
Gareth Stevens Publishing
111 East 14th Street, Suite 349
New York, NY 10003

Produced by Calcium, www.calciumcreative.co.uk
Designed by Paul Myerscough
Edited by Sarah Eason and Laura Waxman
Picture research by Susannah Jayes

Photo credits: Cover: Dreamstime: Scaramax br; Shutterstock: Eyedear bl, Ryan Rodrick Beiler, Styve Reineck bg. Inside: Marcello Casal Jr/ABr: 8bl; Matthias Blume: 42tr; Dreamstime: Anacoimbra 29c, Araraadt 28tr, Galina Barskaya 35tr, Caroline Bomers 14b, Lucian Coman 44bc, Vladimir Melnik 26b, 28bc, Photo360 31tr; Ehsan Iran: 38t; Istockphoto: 33tr, Robert Ellis 7c, Giorgio Fochesato 41tl, Heyoke 34b, Klaas Lingbeek-van Kranen 32t, Chris Pritchard 10b, Matthew Rambo 11tr; Mardetanha: 19t; Hamed Saber: 41br; Shutterstock: Arazu 5tr, Ryan Rodrick Beiler 18bl, Olga Besnard 45tr, Anthony Correia 15tr, P. Fabian 23b, Frontpage 36b, Fulili 22t, Jason and Bonnie Grower 13tr, LeshaBu 21tr, Georgios Kollidas 4bl, MarkauMark 7br, Omer N. Raja 43t, Carsten Reisinger 22cr, SFC 12bl, Ali Mazraie Shadi 27tr, Aleksandar Todorovic 16b, Matt Trommer 42bl, Jon Varsano 30b, Oleg Yarko 37c, Zurijeta 3br, 17t, 24b, 25tr; Taeedxy: 20bc; US Department of Defense: MSGT Deal Toney 6bl; Wikipedia: 39tr; World Economic Forum: Jean-Bernard Sieber 9b.

Printed in the United States of America

CPSIA compliance information: Batch #CS12GS: For further information contact Gareth Stevens, New York, New York at 1-800-542-2595.

CONTENTS

IRAN IN CONFLICT

These days, Iran is rarely out of the headlines. Its nuclear program has led to tensions in the Middle East. Iran has also made enemies by supporting terrorist groups in other countries. At home, there have been violent clashes between those who support Iran's religious leaders and those who want greater democracy.

Ayatollah Khomeini was one of Iran's most influential religious and political leaders.

Iran is a country in the middle of great change. In 1979, religious leader Ayatollah Ruhollah Khomeini led a revolution that overthrew the Iranian shah (king). After the revolution, Iran was ruled by strict Muslim laws about clothing, education, religious beliefs, and other aspects of daily life. Anyone who broke them was severely punished by imprisonment or death.

Although Iranian laws are more relaxed today, many Iranians are demanding even more freedom. Young Iranians in particular are demanding change. Through using the Internet, they are more aware of Western culture and many now wish to enjoy a different type of lifestyle to that lived by older generations.

More than 2,000 years ago, Persepolis was the capital of Persia. This was a vast empire that included Egypt, central Asia, and northern India as well as modern Iran.

A Threat to Peace?

Today, Iran is one of the most powerful countries in the Middle East. Its religious revolution of 1979 inspired many other Muslims in the region. However, Western countries, including the United States and Britain, see Iran as a threat to peace. They have accused the country of trying to make deadly nuclear weapons that could be used against the West. Iran is also hostile to the nearby country of Israel. It trains and supports Muslim terrorists in Lebanon, Palestine, and Iraq to organize attacks against Israel.

NATIONAL PRIDE

Many Iranians are incredibly proud of their traditions. Iran, or Persia as it was once known, was one of the greatest empires of the ancient world. Later, Persia was conquered by Muslim Arabs. Although it became an Islamic country, Iranians still speak their own language, Farsi.

CHAPTER ONE

AN ISLAMIC REPUBLIC

After the revolution in 1979, Ayatollah Khomeini became known as Iran's Supreme Leader. He declared Iran an Islamic Republic. This means that Iran is a democracy in which its people elect a president and government. However, its laws are decided by the supreme leader and other unelected religious leaders.

The hostage crisis in 1979 turned many people in America against Iran. When the hostages returned home, they got a hero's welcome.

The first years of the revolution were violent, and Khomeini's supporters attacked anything to do with the non-Muslim West, such as banks, cinemas, and businesses. In November 1979, Khomeini's supporters stormed the US embassy in Tehran, Iran's capital. They held the US staff hostage for 444 days. This attack angered many people in the United States and resulted in long-lasting tensions between the two nations.

The Iran-Iraq War

In 1980, Iran's neighbor Iraq invaded part of Iran, hoping to take over its valuable oil fields. This led to an eight-year war between the two countries. Although neither side won, 1 million people died in the fighting. The war also led to food and fuel shortages and missile attacks on Tehran.

During the Iran-Iraq War, both sides attacked oil tankers and oil platforms in the Persian Gulf.

AYATOLLAH RUHOLLAH KHOMEINI

Ayatollah Khomeini is one of the most important Iranian figures of the last 100 years. His revolution inspired religious movements in many other Muslim countries. When he died in 1989, 3.5 million people went to his funeral. More than twenty years later, Khomeini is still everywhere. His face appears on Iranian banknotes, and his portrait hangs in every store.

9

New Leaders

When Khomeini died in 1989, the president at the time, Ali Khamenei, became the country's supreme leader. During the 1990s and early 2000s, the next two presidents, Akbar Rafsanjani and Mohammad Khatami, tried to relax some of the stricter laws in Iran.

President Mahmoud Ahmadinejad's plans to develop nuclear power in Iran have led to conflict with the West.

Khatami's support for greater freedoms made him popular with young, often female, citizens who wanted greater freedom. However, although Khatami promised a fresh start for Iran, his reforms were blocked by politicians and lawmakers who wanted to keep to the old Islamic traditions.

President Ahmadinejad

In 2005, Khatami stepped down from power. Mahmoud Ahmadinejad, the former mayor of Tehran, won a surprise victory in the elections that followed. The new president promised to help Iran's poor. However, his aggressive policies created problems both at home and abroad.

Ahmadinejad works closely with the powerful Revolutionary Guards. This military force was set up after the 1979 revolution to protect the country's Islamic system. Since then, it has become a huge power that controls many aspects of daily life, as well as Iran's missiles and nuclear program. The Revolutionary Guards have also been used to crack down on Ahmadinejad's opponents in Iran.

IRAN AND THE IRANIANS

Area of Iran: 636,000 square miles
Population: 77 million people
Capital City: Tehran
Official Language: Farsi
Religion: 97 percent of Iranians are Muslims,
2 percent follow the Baha'i religion. Zoroastrians,
Jews, and Christians also live in Iran.

In the early 2000s, President Mohammad Khatami's attempts to reform Iran were blocked by Iran's religious leaders.

Annual Meeting 2004

LIVING OVERSEAS

Los Angeles, California
June 2001
Dear Hassan,

I'm so excited to be writing to someone in Iran. Although I've heard so much about it from my Iranian parents, I've never been there. When the revolution broke out in 1979, my parents were medical students in the United States. They returned home to join the protests against the shah. But after the revolution, life became very dangerous for anyone who didn't agree with the country's religious laws.

These are the bright lights of downtown Los Angeles. Sometimes we head into town at night to have a meal or to shop.

Iranians in America

Around 2–3 million Iranians fled their homeland after the 1979 revolution. Many were highly educated and skilled professionals such as doctors, engineers, and professors. Today, about 1 million Iranians live in the United States, more than half of them in southern California.

American Iranians protested against President Ahmadinejad's rule in Salt Lake City, Utah, in 2009.

My parents were forced to leave Iran and flee to the United States. Like many Iranian immigrants, they came to Los Angeles—or "Tehrangeles," as we call it. It was very hard for them to leave behind their family and friends. Although they love living in the United States, they sometimes miss their old home. They also worry about our relatives still living in Iran.

We often hear about Iran on television, but most reports show only the bad things that are happening. My mom says this is not the real Iran. She remembers a beautiful country filled with warm, friendly people.

It makes me sad to think that the United States and Iran are rivals. Let's hope that one day our leaders can find a way to bring our two countries closer together.

Rasa

Threats Against Israel

In 2005, Ahmadinejad caused a political storm by saying that Israel would be "wiped off the map." This provoked a hostile reaction from Israel. Like many Muslim leaders, he has argued that the Jewish state of Israel is illegal because it is built on land taken from Arabs.

Iran has also made enemies by sending millions of dollars each year to Muslim terrorist groups across the Middle East. In 2002, US President George W. Bush declared Iran part of an "axis of evil." Over the next few years, several reports claimed that the United States and Israel were planning to attack Iran.

Many of those who took to the streets to protest against President Ahmadinejad's government were young people.

Nuclear Tensions

While US President Barack Obama took a softer approach to Iran, the US government and Israel still feared that Iran was trying to develop nuclear weapons. Iran insisted it was only trying to provide electricity for its people and would not attack another nation. However, its scientists continued to carry out tests on its long-range missiles. Iran also refused to allow international inspectors to tour its nuclear plants. This standoff created a crisis that continues today.

US President George W. Bush often attacked Iran verbally, calling the country "a threat to world peace."

ENEMIES IN THE WEST

Iran's leaders are deeply suspicious of the United States and Britain. In 1953, agents from these two countries overthrew the Iranian Prime Minister Mohammad Mossadeq after he tried to take control of Iran's oil from British and US firms. The United States and Britain then supported the shah for many years before the revolution.

LIVING IN FEAR

Tehran, Iran
April 2002
Dear Rasa,

It was wonderful to get your letter and hear about Los Angeles. I never knew so many Iranians lived there. You are very lucky—many people over here would love to live in the United States. But I guess not everyone there lives like the people we see in Hollywood movies!

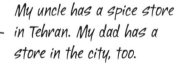

My uncle has a spice store in Tehran. My dad has a store in the city, too.

Reaction to 9/11

After al-Qaeda terrorists attacked New York on September 11, 2001, huge crowds attended candlelit vigils on the streets of Iran. In addition, 60,000 spectators observed a minute's silence in Tehran's soccer stadium. After the attack, US and Iranian officials worked closely to create a new government in Afghanistan, where al-Qaeda's leadership had been based.

Many people in Iran were shocked by the 9/11 attacks on New York City.

Even so, I think things are much harder for ordinary people in Iran. My father is a shopkeeper in Tehran. He has to work very long hours to make a living, even in the summer when it gets so hot. But because US companies are not allowed to trade in Iran, it is difficult to get products from abroad.

Right now, we are also very worried that the United States is going to attack our country. That is difficult to understand. When the United States was attacked by airplanes last September 11, most people here felt nothing but sorrow for the victims. After all, almost every family in Iran knows what it means to lose a loved one. Many of us lost sons or brothers in the war against Iraq. Like people in the United States, we just want to live a peaceful life.

Hassan

CHAPTER TWO

A DIVIDED COUNTRY

Tensions in Iran rose under President Ahmadinejad due to the way his government treated opponents and minorities. Poor Iranians were also angry that few jobs had been created.

Anyone who criticized President Ahmadinejad's government or organized a protest risked being arrested. In addition, the government banned journalists from writing about Iran's problems. The government also persecuted many groups, including women, students, workers, and university professors. Women campaigning for more rights were sent to prison. University professors could not travel abroad. Police arrested thousands of people, often women, for wearing un-Islamic clothing.

Many Iranians work very long hours to make a living, like this man repairing shoes on the streets of Shiraz.

Although teachers are highly respected in Iran, they are badly paid. In 2007, around 150 teachers were arrested for protesting against the government.

Attacks on Baha'is

For many centuries, two major groups of Muslims, the Shia and the Sunni, have been rivals in the Middle East. Although most Iranians are Shia, the country has seen little violence between the two Muslim communities.

However, the Iranian government has persecuted the country's 300,000 Baha'is, who are viewed as enemies of Islam. Members of the Baha'i faith believe all religions share one message and one god. Many Baha'is have been arrested or killed. Iran's government has seized many of their homes, stores, and farms.

IRANIAN JEWS

There are more Jews in Iran than in any other Muslim country. The Jews who live there are free to practice their religion and vote, but Iran's hostility towards Israel has made life difficult for them. Like all Iranians, they are banned from visiting Israel, where many of them have relatives.

Revolution on the Streets

In June 2009, Ahmadinejad won the presidential election for a second time. Many Iranians claimed he had cheated and "stolen" the election from his opponent, Hossein Mousavi. Thousands of Iranians took to the streets in protest against the election. These protests became known as the Green Revolution, due to the color of the flags and ribbons worn by Mousavi's supporters.

The protests were peaceful at first, but then angry crowds broke into stores, smashed windows, and set tires on fire. In a brutal crackdown, government security forces killed dozens of protesters and injured hundreds more. One protester, Neda Soltan, was filmed in her last moments after being shot by a government supporter. The video was posted on the Internet and watched all over the world.

Around 4,000 people were arrested and put in prison. Some of these prisoners were tortured. Others were given very long jail sentences. Since then, Ahmadinejad's opponents have been forced to work in secret, often using social networking sites, especially Twitter. Despite government efforts to control the Internet, protesters manage to keep in touch online.

In 2009, demonstrators in Washington DC held a candlelit vigil to protest against President Ahmadinejad's victory in the Iranian elections.

The opposition leader Hossein Mousavi chose green as his campaign color during the 2009 presidential election and the protests that followed.

OTHER PROTESTS

The protests in 2009 were not the first under Ahmadinejad. Two years earlier, thousands of teachers demonstrated against low wages and were attacked by government forces. Many teachers were later fired, forced to quit, or sent to prison. Security forces have also violently broken up protests by workers at electronic and textile factories.

UNDERSTANDING OUR CULTURE

Los Angeles, California
December 2005
Dear Hassan,

It has been a strange couple of years. After the 9/11 attacks, many people here did not have good feelings about Iran. Some of the other girls at school started to tease me. They thought that all Iranians were Muslims and did not understand that most Muslims disagreed with the 9/11 attacks.

When I told them that I was a Baha'i, they'd never heard of my religion. They felt bad when I explained how Iranian Baha'is have been badly treated.

These are the ruins of a Baha'i cemetery destroyed by government forces in Iran.

Iranian Calendar

The Baha'i religion is linked to Zorastrianism, an ancient Persian religion. Iran's calendar goes back to ancient Zoroastrian times and is based on the movements of the sun rather than the moon. The Iranian new year, called Noruz, begins in March. It is celebrated with a festival that lasts up to two weeks.

The ringstone symbol is often used on Baha'i rings, book covers, and paintings.

It's one of main reasons why my parents moved to the United States. Mom told me recently that Baha'is are still being put in prison, just because of their beliefs. From what I've heard, the religious leaders in Iran haven't given anyone there a lot of freedom, especially women and girls.

The other day I saw a report on television that Iran is trying to make nuclear weapons. People here are really scared that Iran might use them to attack Israel or other countries in the Middle East. But I can't believe Iran's leaders really want to start a war.

Please write soon and tell me how things are for you.

Rasa

A number of Kurdish politicians and writers have been arrested and executed by the Iranian government, leading to protests by Kurdish people.

Iran's Ethnic Groups

About half of all Iranians are of Persian descent and most are Shia Muslims. The rest of the country is a mix of different ethnic groups and tribes, including Lurs, Kurds, Arabs, Turkomans, Azeris, and Baluchs. Many of these smaller groups live close to Iran's borders.

IRAN'S FLAG

The green in Iran's flag represents Islam, the white is for peace, and the red stands for the bravery and loyalty of Iran's people. The red symbol in the middle of the flag is the word "Allah," meaning God.

Ahmadinejad's government, which is mostly Persian, wants Iran's ethnic groups to be more like the rest of Iranian society. Many ethnic communities are not allowed to speak their own languages in schools. It is also hard for them to get good jobs or a good education.

Ethnic Violence

Over the years, these ethnic groups have often held protests. Armed Kurdish fighters have attacked police stations and military bases, Turkish people have rioted, and Arabs have blown up oil pipelines. In the future, Iran's ethnic groups could cause even more trouble for the government.

At the same time, many ethnic communities are losing their old traditions. In the last 20 years, many people have moved from farms and villages to cities, where there are better jobs, education, and health care. These days, nearly two in three Iranians live in cities, but the move has made life difficult for some tribal communities.

Many Kurds live in western Iran. Many villages here suffer from a lack of basic services such as drinking water and health care.

CLAMPDOWN

Tehran, Iran
July 2007
Dear Rasa,
   It was very interesting to hear about your Baha'i faith. I think everyone should follow your belief that there should only be one religion and one god. It would make the world a much more peaceful place. By the way, did you know that Islam comes from the Arabic word "salaam," meaning peace?

Women in Iran are expected to wear clothes that cover their face and body.

Dress Code

Iran's so-called "morality police" make sure all Iranians wear strict Islamic clothing. That means dressing modestly, especially for women. Morality police wait outside shopping malls and crowded streets, warning pedestrians and drivers if they are showing too much hair or wearing clothes that are too tight. If people argue with them, they are arrested and taken to the police station.

Few men wear ties in Iran as they are a symbol of the West.

Things are very unsettled in Iran at the moment. The police are a lot stricter since President Ahmadinejad came to power. My uncle's bookstore got into trouble for selling books from Western nations. Then police stopped our neighbor for wearing brightly colored clothes. My father was on the Internet the other day when, suddenly, the website he was looking at vanished. The government must have blocked it. It's getting harder and harder to find out what is going on in the rest of the world.

Recently there have also been several attacks on police forces in Iran, and even a bomb attack on people visiting a mosque. People worry that, if the violence gets worse, Iran could have the same problems as Iraq, where different groups are fighting for power.

Hassan

CHAPTER THREE

DAILY LIFE

Life for ordinary people in Iran has not been easy since the revolution in 1979, especially for poor Iranians. The country's political turmoil has made life very uncertain for everyone. Government corruption also is a major problem. Without the right connections, it can be very hard to get a job. However, Iranians live a much better life than their neighbors in war-torn Iraq and Afghanistan.

Religion is a very important part of daily life. Large mosques dominate the skyline of many Iranian towns and cities. The Shah Mosque in Isfahan is 400 years old.

For many decades, Iran depended on its rich oil fields for its wealth. However, after the revolution, the country's economy suffered. First, the war with Iraq created large debts. Over the next 15 years, the United States increased sanctions against Iran. This meant that US companies were banned from investing in Iran or from buying and selling goods in the country. The sanctions do not stop goods from coming into Iran, they just cost more and take longer to arrive.

Although Iran's economy has grown slowly in recent years, the lack of jobs is a major problem, especially for young, educated people. As a result, young Iranians often live with their parents well into their twenties. Many skilled workers and businesspeople are leaving the country.

The soil in many parts of Iran is not good for growing crops, so the government has to buy large amounts of wheat from other countries.

ENERGY SUPERPOWER

One reason why the world takes such an interest in Iran is because it sits on a sea of oil and gas. It has the world's third-largest oil reserves and the world's second-largest gas reserves. It has been called an energy superpower.

Women in Iran

The Islamic revolution brought big changes for Iran's women, who were suddenly expected to live traditional lives as wives and mothers. They are also required to wear the hijab, clothing that covers the whole body except for the hands and face. Outside the home, Iranian women are separated from men in public places such as mosques, schools, parks, and beaches. In cities, they are expected to ride at the back of a bus.

Since 1979, women have made some progress, thanks to efforts by reformers. They can drive their own cars and have successful careers. There are also several female lawmakers in Iran's parliament.

Iranians living in the West have protested against the strict dress code for women in Iran.

In Iran, men and women are often separated in public, such as in mosques. There are also women-only parks, trains, and banks.

Women only واگن ویژه بانوان

Education

Iranians value education, and the standard of teaching is very high. All children, boys and girls, go to school between the ages of 6 and 14, and over 1 million Iranians go to college each year. In recent times, more girls than boys have enrolled in universities. Despite this, women can find it hard to get a job.

Although girls in Iran have the same education as boys, it is often much harder for them to find a job after they leave school or university.

IRANIAN FAMILIES

Few people live alone in Iran, and when young Iranians leave home, they often live close to their parents. Islamic law allows an Iranian man to have as many as four wives. Most men, however, have only one wife. After the revolution, families were encouraged to have as many children as possible to make Iran more powerful. As a result, Iran's population has doubled since the 1970s.

CAUGHT BETWEEN ENEMIES

Los Angeles, California
April 2008
Dear Hassan,
    After your last letter, I've been thinking about you and your family. The bombing campaign in Iran must be very scary on top of all your other worries. Although it has been several years since 9/11, Americans are still afraid of another terrorist attack. A friend of my father's, who was in New York at the time, is still nervous about taking the subway.

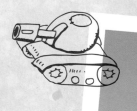

It hardly ever snows here in Los Angeles—the weather gets much colder in Tehran in winter.

Sanctions

One of the effects sanctions are having on Iran is forcing foreign investors to pull out of the country. Many Iranian companies have gone bankrupt, while large billboards that once advertised watches or cars are now empty. Spare parts for airplanes are now on the list of international products banned from Iran. Some fear this will lead to more air disasters as Iran's airplanes get older.

Since the revolution, there have been no direct flights between the United States and Iran.

There is still a lot in the news about Iran's nuclear program and more US sanctions. Iranians living in the United States often feel like we are caught in the middle. We hear lots of stories about people getting locked up, so we support tough US action against Iran's leaders. But we also realize that sanctions hurt ordinary Iranians like your father.

So often, leaders from our two countries exchange angry words rather than seek out ways to work together. Iranian Americans would like to help—most of us have relatives still in Iran. But it is hard to know how. When my dad sent some money to his cousins, they got into trouble with the police.

Mountain resorts in Iran are popular places for skiing. Some mountains in the northern part of the country have snow all year long.

The Friendly Face of Iran

Television reports usually focus on Iran's problems, but this is just one side of modern Iran. Visitors to the country are often shocked by what they find. Despite the tensions between Iran and the West, the Iranian tradition of hospitality means that foreigners are made to feel very welcome. By nature, Iranians are very inquisitive. They are interested in the world and love to chat with visitors or discuss politics.

In the summer, the weather in many parts of Iran is so hot that most stores and offices close during the afternoon. People often sleep after lunch and go out in the evening, when the air is cooler. There are parks where children can play until midnight—it's too hot to sleep before then!

Strict Islamic rules live alongside a modern society. Kissing in public is banned, but young couples might hold hands as they stroll through one of Tehran's parks. Although modern music and dancing are officially forbidden, musicians and singers perform popular Iranian and Western hits in public. Many foreign television shows are also banned, but satellite dishes can be seen on many rooftops.

After the revolution, American movies were banned, so Iranian moviegoers mainly watch films made in Iran.

LEISURE TIME

The weekend in Iran is Thursday and Friday. Iranians often like to spend it in large groups, whether hiking up a mountain, meeting for coffee, or having a dinner party at home. Many Iranians, especially men, are huge soccer fans. European games are often broadcast on Iranian state television.

A DOUBLE LIFE

Tehran, Iran
May 2009
Dear Rasa,

Thanks for all your kind words. There is great excitement in Iran now because of the upcoming election to choose a new president. Many of us are hoping President Ahmadinejad will not get elected a second time. A new government could lead to big changes in our country, such as more jobs or better relations with the United States.

Getting a modern haircut in Iran is difficult, as the police have closed down many barber shops and hairdressers that copy Western styles.

Looking Good

Iranians love to look good! They take a lot of time with their appearance. While Western fashions are often worn to private parties, some designers also copy ancient Persian fashions. Since the 1979 revolution, many thousands of Iranians have also had plastic surgery, both men and women. Nose jobs are especially popular.

At home, many Iranian women wear Western fashions.

Every night, thousands of young people take to the streets of Tehran and sing campaign songs for Ahmadinejad's opponent, Hossein Mousavi. We hear that things are different outside the cities, though. In the countryside, many people would prefer to keep things the way they are. They don't want a new government.

These days, more and more Iranians are living a double life. On the streets, everyone is very careful about how they look and behave. Women and girls follow the rules about Islamic clothing and cover up. They look very traditional. But at home, everything changes. They wear jeans, put on makeup, watch American movies, and listen to Western music.

I think if Americans knew how much Iranians love the West, they would be shocked!

Hussan

CHAPTER FOUR

IRAN'S FUTURE

Although Iran has its problems, things are not as bad as some television reports in the West suggest. Sanctions have made it hard to do business in Iran, but the country still has large reserves of oil and gas. At the same time, protests against governments in neighboring countries have sparked hope among Iranians that change is possible.

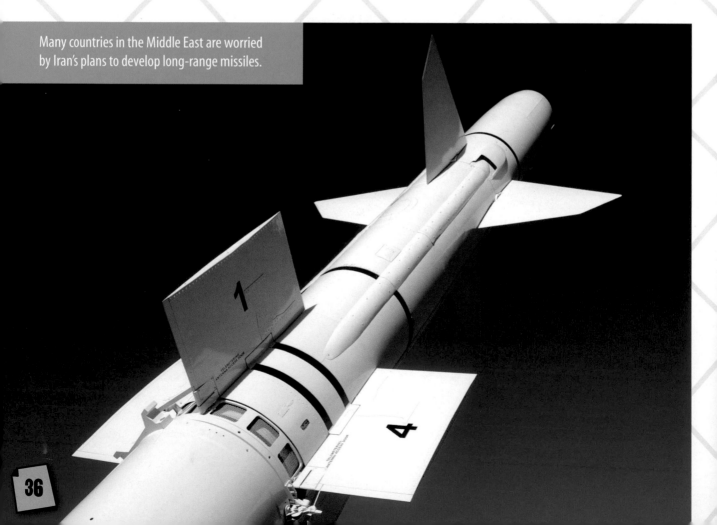

Many countries in the Middle East are worried by Iran's plans to develop long-range missiles.

The angry revolt against President Ahmadinejad after his re-election in 2009 seemed to die out when Iran's security forces crushed the protests. However, in 2011, there were more large antigovernment rallies. The demonstrators were inspired by the mass protests in Egypt, Tunisia, Libya, and other Muslim countries. Although Iran's security forces quickly ended the rallies, the protests showed that many Iranians still desired reform.

Meanwhile, tensions between Iran and the West remain high, due mainly to Iran's nuclear program. If Iran's secrecy over its nuclear program continues, the United States or Israel may decide to attack the country before it becomes a nuclear power. However, if the United States offered Iran a good deal, its leaders might be willing to give up their nuclear program. The world watches and waits to see what the outcome will be.

The United States has used spy planes such as unmanned drones to gather information on Iran's nuclear program.

SPY PLANE

In 2011, the Iranian army captured a US remote-controlled plane, or drone, which was flying deep inside Iran. The plane was probably spying on nuclear plants and missile sites in Iran. The United States has asked for the drone back, but Iran has refused to return it.

Iran's security forces, especially the Republic Guards, are very powerful. They have often been used to break up demonstrations by groups that oppose the government.

Living in Fear

Today, most Iranians are still afraid to speak out against the government. Those who do, such as Nobel Peace Prize winner Shirin Ebadi, are forced to flee the country. Iran's courts are full of Iranians who have been accused of plotting against the government. Many anti-government newspapers have also been closed and their editors jailed. Freedom of speech is impossible.

There is little hope of reform under President Ahmadinejad, but Iran is a youthful country that is constantly changing. More than 40 percent of Iranians are under the age of 15. Who knows what changes the next generation will bring?

Terrorist Attacks in Iran

In recent years, there has been growing unrest among Iran's ethnic groups. In southeastern Iran, an armed group of Baluchs, known as Jundallah, have carried out numerous bombings and attacks. These have included an attack on a Shiite mosque in the city of Zahedan, as well as a bombing that killed 42 people—the deadliest in Iran in more than 20 years. There has also been heavy fighting along the Iraqi border, where Kurdish fighters have carried out raids on Iranian soldiers posted there.

This is an illustration from a translation of Omar Khayyam's *Rubaiyat* by Edward Fitzgerald.

SPEAKING OUT

Iran is well known for its poetry and writing. Its most famous poet is Omar Khayyam. His collection of poems, known as the *Rubaiyat*, has been translated into many languages. However, in recent years, Iranian writers are not as free to express themselves. Many have been punished for criticizing the government.

LOST HOPE

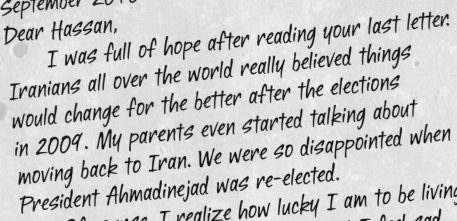

Los Angeles, California
September 2010
Dear Hassan,

I was full of hope after reading your last letter. Iranians all over the world really believed things would change for the better after the elections in 2009. My parents even started talking about moving back to Iran. We were so disappointed when President Ahmadinejad was re-elected.

Of course, I realize how lucky I am to be living in a country like the United States. But I feel sad when I remember what is going on in Iran. For days, we watched the Green Revolution protests on television. We felt very proud of all the young Iranians who wanted their voices to be heard. We also watched in horror when the security forces attacked them.

It feels good telling you all this because most of the kids at my school don't really know what is going on in Iran. Thanks to your letters, I feel I know a lot more about the real Iran. From what you say, there is every reason for our countries to be friends. Who knows, one day I may even be able to visit you in Tehran.

Your friend,

Rasa

The Basij

During the crackdown, local militias, known as Basij helped to attack antigovernment protesters. They used weapons such as daggers, axes, clubs, and even guns, and wore ordinary clothes to hide among the protesters. There are 5 million Basij members in Iran, with leaders based in mosques in every village and town.

Protesters claimed that President Ahmadinejad had "stolen" the election. When they took to the streets in Tehran, they were attacked by local militias known as the Basij.

Life Goes On

Recent government reforms in Iran have raised the price of basics such as fuel, water, and bread. However, the government has also been handing out cash payments to help millions of the poorest Iranians. In addition, it is trying to encourage the growth of private banks that can support struggling businesses.

Tehran is one of the smoggiest cities in the world. Air pollution in the capital kills thousands of people each year.

Iran is one of the few countries in the world that has not been badly affected by the banking crisis of 2008.

There have been big improvements in education and health care in the last 30 years, too. Meanwhile, metro lines and fast bus lanes in Tehran are helping to reduce smog in one of the world's most polluted cities.

Opening Doors

Despite these positive changes, Iran remains very isolated. Even Muslim nations such as Saudi Arabia are scared by Iran's nuclear ambitions. If Iran can find a way to work with the outside world, foreign investors could help rebuild the country. Despite the country's strict Islamic culture, many ordinary Iranians would welcome the West with open arms if they could.

Many Iranians communicate with the outside world via the Internet.

A CHANGING WORLD

Although the Iranian government is doing its best to control the media, in many ways it is fighting a losing battle. The spread of satellite television gives many Iranian homes access to international news channels. Since 2000, the Internet has also grown faster in Iran than in any other Middle Eastern country. By 2009, almost half of all Iranians were Internet users. There are also more than 100,000 active Iranian blogs, making Farsi the second most popular language among bloggers worldwide.

ALL CHANGE!

Tehran, Iran
December 2011
Dear Rasa,

Don't give up hope! Yes, our strict laws can make Iran a difficult and dangerous place to live. And no one knows what is going to happen, so it is hard to make plans for the future. However, one thing is for sure: things are changing fast.

Iran is getting more modern every day. There are now fast food restaurants and shopping malls in many parts of Tehran—just like in the United States. Women play sports, such as soccer and golf, and more and more Iranians are going on vacations abroad to countries like Turkey and Malaysia.

Many Iranians are huge soccer fans and dream that one day Iran will win the World Cup!

Christmas in Iran

Images of Santa Claus are now seen on the streets of Tehran. Christmas trees, cards, and decorations are also on sale. However, a real tree can cost up to $1,000! On Christmas Day, Iranian Christians worship at one of the city's many churches.

Of Iranian descent, tennis player Aravane Rezai is one of the best in the world.

There they can enjoy pop concerts by singers and dancers banned in Iran. They also get a taste of what it is like to live in another country. Don't forget, Iranians love to have fun!

A new kind of car here is the first to be made completely in Iran, and we have also sent our first satellite into space, the Ovid. I would like to be an astronaut one day.

From space, I'll look down on the United States and remember my friend in Los Angeles, who hoped for peace just like me.

Hassan

GLOSSARY

al-Qaeda a terrorist group that was responsible for the 9/11 attacks on New York City in 2001

Ayatollah a high-ranking religious leader among Shia Muslims

Baha'i a religion that began in Persia (Iran) during the nineteenth century, which has often come into conflict with Islam

Basij local armed groups based in mosques in towns and villages across Iran

democracy a form of government where people take part, usually by voting in elections for the politicans who will make decisions on their behalf

demonstation another word for a protest, when a large group of people gather together to speak out about something they think is wrong

drone an unmanned remote-controlled aircraft

economy all the goods and services in a country, the things that make money or move it from place to place

election when people vote to choose a politician or leader

ethnic group people who share the same culture

Green Revolution a nickname for the protest movement in Iran following the 2009 elections

hijab traditional Islamic clothing that covers the whole body apart from the face and hands

hostage a person taken by force and kept until certain demands are met

immigrant someone who leaves their home country to start a new life in another country

Islam a religion based on the teachings of the Prophet Muhammad and a belief in one god, Allah. The main religion in the Middle East, North Africa, and Central and South Asia.

mosque Islamic places of worship that are often also community centers

nuclear program building nuclear plants to produce energy or create weapons

persecution the harsh and unfair treatment of a person or group

rebel someone who fights against something, often a government or other authority

revolution when violence is used to overthrow one government and replace it with another

sanctions putting pressure on a government, such as stopping it from buying and selling goods from other countries

shah the former king of Iran

terrorist a person or group who carries out violent acts against civilians to achieve a political goal

FOR MORE INFORMATION

Books

Bauer, Brandy. *Iran: A Question and Answer Book*. Mankato, MN: Fact Finders, 2005.

Schemenauer, Elma. *Welcome to Iran*. Mankato, MN: Child's World, 2008.

Simmons, Walter. *Exploring Countries: Iran*. Minneapolis, MN: Bellwether Media, 2011.

Yip, Dora. *Welcome to My Country: Iran*. London: Franklin Watts, 2006.

Websites

kids.nationalgeographic.com/kids/places/find/iran/
Find out more about Iran and its culture.

www.intercaspian.com
Take a look at some amazing photographs of Iran.

kids.yahoo.com/reference/world-factbook/country/ir--Iran
Visit this website for statistics and facts.

www.enchantedlearning.com/asia/iran
Read key facts about Iran.

Publisher's note to educators and parents: Our editors have carefully reviewed these websites to ensure that they are suitable for students. Many websites change frequently, however, and we cannot guarantee that a site's future contents will continue to meet our high standards of quality and educational value. Be advised that students should be closely supervised whenever they access the Internet.

INDEX